NILS MARTELLUCCI

LIFE AND WORKS OF

MICHELANGELO

IN FLORENCE

TRANSLATED BY
TIMOTHY PATERSON

BONECHI - EDIZIONI " IL TURISMO „ - FLORENCE
5, VIA DEI RUSTICI

Perhaps no famous artist has had so many portraits made of him as Michelangelo. However, the majority of them are but copies of the few originals mentioned by Giorgio Vasari, his contemporary, who cites the portrait painted by Giuliano Bugiardini for Ottaviano dei Medici, that by Jacopo del Conte which, an excellent likeness of the sculptor, is reproduced in this volume, and finally the fine one in bronze by Daniele Ricciarelli da Volterra.

As regards the latter bust in bronze, Michelangelo in a number of letters mentions that Daniele Ricciarelli made a total of three: two for his nephew, Lionardo, and one for himself. Following the death of Daniele, his assistants cast a further copy at the request of Diomede Leoni, a close friend of Michelangelo.

Of the foregoing busts, it is uncertain whether the one in the National Museum is the first of the series, though it is known that it once belonged to Antonio del Francese from Castel Durante, Michelangelo's last servant, who later presented it to the Duke of Urbino in 1570. Furthermore, a number of copies made from the medal by Leone Leoni, on a par with the fine one by Santarelli, are still known to exist.

MICHELANGELO BUONARROTI

In the year 1475, Messer Lodovico Buonarroti noted down in his diary the following passage: «I recall how on this sixth day of March a male child was born unto me, being born on Monday morning four or five hours before daybreak, I being Mayor of Caprese, and was baptized with the name of Michelagnolo in the Church of St. John».

With these few words, typical of a scrupulous, pedantic bureaucrat, the father of the great artist thus announces the happy event, though omitting to mention his wife, Francesca, who, according to Vasari, was an « honest, noble woman » who gave birth to the child under a « fatal and felicitous star ».

As regards the aristocratic origin of the Buonarroti-Simoni family, it is unnecessary to dwell at length on the subject. Suffice it to say that all his life Michelangelo was intensely proud of his ancestry and jealously guarded the documents proving his relationship to the Counts of Canossa. Even though his overwhelming genius rightly caused him to be defined « divine and terrible », in daily life and practical matters, in similar fashion to the rest of his family, he was both wise and sensible, lived simply and soon learned the value of money.

He had four brothers: the eldest, Lionardo, was a mystic, who, having heard Girolamo Savonarola preach his sermons, took holy orders, becoming a Dominican monk; his second brother, Buonarroto, was a merchant; his third, Giovan Simone, travelled the world in search of adventure and was considered the black sheep of the austere family; and, finally, Sigismondo, who started life as a soldier and ended his days as a peasant at Settignano.

Michelangelo's father was stingy, to such an extent that he inspired little love in his five sons. Yet by nature he was by no means wicked or bad; on the contrary, according to his fellows, he was a « man of holy habits ». He once wrote to the Magnificent Lorenzo the following words: « ... I have never practised any trade or art, though up till now have always lived upon my modest income... I am unable to do anything but read and write... ».

His mother, Francesca, died young, at the age of forty-two, when Michelangelo was still but a boy. As a babe in swaddling-bands he was not suckled by her, this task being entrusted to a wet-nurse from Settignano. He later lived with a step-mother, who was perhaps cold and authoritarian towards him.

The artist never spoke of his mother, though we often come across her in his magnificent works, almost as if he remmembered with filial nostalgia her presence, however remote, during the early days of his solitary childhood.

In his biography of Michelangelo, first published in 1555, Ascanio Condivi, his favourite pupil, faithfully describes the features and physical appearance of his beloved master. « Michelangelo is of sound constitution », he writes; « in body muscular and bony rather than fat and fleshy; above all healthy, both by nature and through excercising his body, as well as by his continence in the pleasures of Venus and restraint in eating, even though as a child he was weak and sickly and twice ill in manhood. His face is of good colour. Of average height, he is broad of shoulder, the rest of his body well built and suitably proportioned, though somewhat on the thin side. His head and forehead are square, his nose is slightly bent and flattened, this being due to a punch received as a child from one Torrigiano, a brutal, arrogant man. Yet his nose, flattened as it is, is nevertheless proportionate to his forehead and the rest of his face. His lips are thin, though the lower lip is somewhat thicker than its upper neighbour, while his chin blends well with the aforementioned parts. His eyelashes have but few hairs; his eyes are small, of horny colour, yet mottled with light blue and yellowish streaks; his ears are of the correct size; his hair is black, as is his beard. Being now in the seventy-ninth year, his hair is shaggy and hoary with age, while his beard is parted in the middle, four or five fingers in length, though not very thick ».

The great sculptor first saw the light of day in the small castle atop a hill in the country town of Caprese, in the Casentino district, not far from Verna, Chiusi and the Tiber Valley. Even at the present time the inhabitants of the town and surrounding area honour with respect and veneration the memory of their illustrious fellow citizen.

On April 1, 1488, Michelangelo was entrusted by his father to the care of David and Domenico del Ghirlandaio, his aim being that the two worthy painters should teach the thirteen-year-old boy the art of painting. Michelangelo was to have stayed with the Ghirlandaio brothers for a period of three years, following, which the young apprentice was to receive the sum of ninety-six lire. Prior to this date, it is almost certain that the lad was not kept idle by his parents. It is known that he had learnt the rudiments of grammar under the tuition of Francesco da Urbino, though it was already clear that by natural inclination his ultimate calling was to be very different, and also that the irksome study of Latin was ill-suited to his lively, yet peevish character. His greatest desire was to frequent the company of artists, drawing and reproducing under their guidance the living things he saw about him, to such an extent as to force his surly father to give in and send him to the school of the brothers Ghirlandaio.

However, as matters turned out, he remained with the latter little less than a year, drawing no benefit whatever from the teaching of his able masters. In fact, conversing amicably one day with his friend and favourite pupil, Ascanio Condivi, he chanced to say: « ... Domenico was to be greatly appreciated in both his art and manners, though I profited by neither of these ».

On the other hand, it cannot be denied that Domenico del Ghirlandaio and his brothers were esteemed and considered the finest artists in Florence at the time. In proof of their fame and skill is their being commissioned, among other things, to decorate with frescoes the large choir in the Church of Santa Maria Novella.

Giovanni Papini, in his *Life of Michelangelo*, is of the opinion that critics in general tend to unjustly exaggerate their judgment of the unfortunate Domenico, and furthermore wholly disagrees with both Ruskin and Berenson, who, though praising his technique as a painter, consider him superficial and without personality.

As regards the envy shown by the master towards his young, promising pupil, this could well be attributed to the mere imagination of his contemporaries and no more. Yet enlarged and supported by further evidence and episodes, both pleasant and unpleasant, Domenico's envy towards Michelangelo is often mentioned in works — many of them modern — dealing with Michelangelo.

In fact, following a closer examination of contemporary documents, it results that Michelangelo did not leave Domenico, but rather it was Domenico who sent him to one Bertoldo, for the simple reason that the Magnificent Lorenzo had asked the latter to send him « ... any excellent youth who showed an inclination to sculpture and already knew, or was willing to learn, the art of fashioning rounded figures, both in clay and marble ».

It is of interest to mention a canvas painted by Michelangelo, while still in the care of Domenico del Ghirlandaio, representing *St. Anthony being beaten by demons.* In this small painting were manifest strange and monstrous figures of devils, apart from the effigy of the Saint himself, executed by Michelangelo « with such diligence and perfection as to arouse from then on the admiration of the whole world ».

Unfortunately, the masterpiece was lost during the centuries that followed, though it is known that Michelangelo drew ispiration for it from a print by Martin Schoengauer called « the German », a skilled engraver of the time.

Michelangelo was thus dispatched to the Medici Garden, in St. Mark's Square, where the Magnificent Lorenzo had gathered together all manner of ancient, beautiful sculptures, entrusting them to the care of Bertoldo, beloved follower of Donatello, that he might inculcate into the youths present there the love of art. And so Michelangelo, having laid aside his brushes, was able to try his hand at sculpture for the first time, carving in due course the famous *Mask of a Faun,* which, apart from being praised by his biographers, immensely pleased the Magnificent Lorenzo. The following passage is recounted by Condivi and later repeated by Vasari: «He set about copying the head of an old, wrinkled faun. Having seen the sculptured head, the Magnificent Lorenzo was greatly astonished, and pleasantly making sport of Michelangelo as he was wont to do, said: « Thou oughtst to know. that old men never have all their teeth ». It seemed to Michelangelo that he was speaking the truth; so he struck a tooth from the mouth of the faun and bored through the gum in such a fashion as to make it appear that the tooth had indeed dropped out. Having taken note of the simplicity and goodness of Michelangelo, the Magnificent Lorenzo laughed heartily and at length, and having made up his mind to help him, sent for Lodovico his father and told him that he would like to take the boy into his care as one of his own sons, whereupon Lodovico granted his wish ». And thus the Magnificent Lorenzo dei Medici was for Michelangelo, to use his own words, « *in loco di patre* », « as a father ». Under the guidance of Bertoldo, the young artist was assiduous, diligent and ever ready to learn, though was prone to bouts of melancholy in his youth, irascible in his old age and on the whole little given to speaking. Furthermore, he was deeply fond of music and poetry, and treated on equal terms popes, princes and sovereigns. Caustic of speech and swift to judge his fellows, he loved solitude and despised the luxury of a vain, comfortable life.

He always considered himself a true Florentine, his mother having conceived him while in Florence, and breathed the air of her streets and surrounding hills until the age of twenty. He kept well clear of politics and when at a loss as to how to act in times of strife, fled from danger, as often as not imaginary.

Following the death of Lorenzo the Magnificent in 1492, Michelangelo was forced to leave the latter's sumptuous family palace in the Via Larga, today Via Cavour, for his parent's modest home; and deprived of guidance and now utterly alone, he was beset by fits of sadness and depression.

Having carved in high relief the *Battle of the Centaurs*, he next created in 1492 a stupendous figure of *Hercules* that went to France and was there unfortunately lost. On January 20, 1494, he completed a fine *Giant of the Snows*, commissioned by Piero dei Medici for the courtyard of the Medici Palace.

Once Piero dei Medici, a man totally lacking in common sense and shrewdness, had duly been removed from office, Michelangelo travelled to Bologna where he was received by Gian Francesco Aldrovandi, who commissioned him to carve an *angel bearing a candelabrum,* or branched candlestick, to replace the one missing from the Ark of St. Dominic. A year after his arrival in Bologna, he returned to Florence where he set to work on a statue of *St. Giovannino.* Following this, he made a marvellous figure of *Cupid* that was later acquired by the Cardinal of San Giorgio.

On June 25, 1496, he was in Rome, where ha carved a *Bacchus* for Jacopo Galli. The statue aroused the admiration of all and sundry, especially that of Cardinal Jean de la Groslaye de Villiers, who commissioned from him the famous *Pietà*, now in St. Peter's, the sole work of Michelangelo to receive the artist's autograph. It is interesting to note that at the time the sculptor was aged but twenty-four. The group is all the more surprising as it clearly indicates the profound knowledge Michelangelo had of human anatomy.

A well-known Tuscan author in his biography of Michelangelo throws further light on the matter when, referring to the assiduousness and untiring energy with which the great artist applied himself to his studies of anatomy, he wrote: « As was often his custom during his lifetime, he would take refuge among the dead, almost as if to overcome the thought of death by keeping the company of corpses ».

On the other hand, Vasari, less of a poet, has this to say: « By stripping the skin off bodies in order to study the intricacies of anatomy, he began to perfect his knowledge of drawing that later became profound ». The question is often asked just how and when the vocation for the arts in general and sculpture in particular was first manifest in Michelangelo. It is difficult to give an answer, in that he was a born artist, and it is therefore impossible to trace the origin of the talent bestowed on him by God and Nature. In him faults were transformed into virtues, and the solitary spirit he was, he succeeded in excelling above all his renowned contemporaries, having in him that fire which is the gift of but a few and which is found solely in the greatest of universal geniuses. Michelangelo himself, on being put the same question by his friend Vasari, deftly eluded the issue by replying: « Dear Giorgio, if I have no intelligence and wits, these I duly acquired by being born in the subtle air of a village near your native town of Arezzo; and likewise I drew from the milk of my wet-nurse's breast the mallet and chisels with which I carve my statues ».

The year 1501 marks the beginning of further trials and tribulations for Michelangelo, which, though they were long-lasting and caused him much anxiety, he nevertheless succeeded in overcoming, completing at the same time his gigantic statue of *David*. The latter, a work of titanic, noble dimensions, was set free from a block of marble rough-hewn by one Agostino di Luccio prior to being sent to Michelangelo. A work of incomparable beauty, the likes of *David* had never been seen before and seemed to have been created by a divine, hidden force, rather than by the hand of man. Michelangelo was acclaimed an artist of prodigious qualities and was even attributed with supernatural faculties for having « resuscitated one who was already dead ».

During the same period, he painted for Agnolo and Maddalena Doni-Strozzi a *Holy Family,* defined by the illustrious Pietro Selvatico as a work « more·than profane »

in content, yet on the whole executed with outstanding « cleanliness and wisdom ». Michelangelo was so pleased with the result that he used the same subject in another *tondo*, carved this time in marble and as a *bas-relief*. Following this, he was commissioned to carve a *St. Matthew* and was duly issued with a second block of marble by the Opera di Santa Maria del Fiore (Cathedral Works Department), the first having been given him for his statue of David. However, the work was never completed and today may be seen in the Gallery of the Academy. At the end these of efforts, perhaps tired and discouraged, he left off working at his sculptures and retreated into the silence of his home, where he once again took up his favourite books and delved into the mysteries of the *Divine Comedy,* by his favourite Dante, as well as into the Holy Scriptures. Yet he did not remain idle for long and, in 1504, drew his cartoon for the *Battle of Cascina,* to be later painted in the form of frescoes on the walls of the Council Chamber in the Palazzo Vecchio. The cartoon, described by Benvenuto Cellini as a « school for the world » on account of its perfection, was later transferred to the Medici Palace, in the Via Larga, where in due course, through carelessness and neglect — a typically Italian malady — it was cut up into sections, torn and eventually reduced to shreds, with the result that of it nothing remains today.

Summoned to Rome by Pope Julius II, he was commissioned by the latter to make him a sepulchre without equal throughout the world. But Michelangelo, angered by matters of money during his transactions with the Pope, returned to Florence, crying out: « Tell His Holiness that should he again seek my services, be must look for me elsewhere »! However, they soon made peace and the Pope once more summoned

Michelangelo, this time to Bologna, where he ordered him to portray his likeness in a gigantic statue. On completion, the statue was cast in bronze and later buried by the artful citizens of Bologna. Disinterred some years later, the metal was melted down and remade into a cannon which, according to the historians, proved in war to be a « mighty weapon ».

Having again quarrelled with the Pope, he was forced by the latter to decorate with frescoes the vaulting of the Sistine Chapel, a work that turned out to be a masterpiece without equal. According to some, it was completed in 1509, after only twenty months, though others give the year 1512, after forty-eight months. The last word, however, fell to Michelangelo, who remarked laconically: « The work of the fresco is not my art ». He was paid three thousand ducats for his labours, out of which he spent twenty-five for the purchase of paints. Michelangelo executed the work without any help and even prepared the necessary materials on his own. According to Condivi, the Pope « loved him with all his heart, lavishing on him more care and jealousy than any other living person ».

Following Pope Julius II's death and the re-entry of the Medici into Florence, the son of Lorenzo the Magnificent was elected Pope, taking the name of Leone X. The latter being a young man who had been brought up amid the elegant splendours of palace life, Michelangelo was duly commissioned to complete work on the Church of San Lorenzo, and, later, on May 4, 1519, to build the New Sacristy, in which he gave free reign to his imagination, the likes of which had never been seen before, and which to this day has been surpassed by none other.

After the death of Leone X and that of Hadrian VI, Clement VII dei Medici was duly elected to the Papal throne. Much against his will, Michelangelo found himself being forced to serve the latter Pope, a man of ambiguous nature who, through his foolishness, brought about the Sack of Rome and plunged Florence into war. During the memorable siege, Michelangelo helped fortify the walls of the city from which, among swift-changing events, he fled twice. Yet he was soon to return, once all bitterness had been laid aside, and took up his work again. Meanwhile the Florentines had lost all hopes of victory following the death of Francesco Ferrucci and the betrayal of Malatesta Baglioni.

On September 20, 1534, by way of the Porta al Prato, Michelangelo fled from Florence, and passing through Pescia and Pisa, finally reached Rome. For a further thirty years until his death in 1564, Florence was for him but a memory full of painful regrets, almost an unattainable dream. He left behind him not only his father, Lodovico, and his best-loved brother, Buonarroto, but also the places where he had spent the greater part of his infancy, youth and mature years, abandoning there the finest fruits of his troubled life. And then in the hovel in the poor Roman quarter of Macel dei Corvi, he was suddenly alone, staring with open eyes at the squalor around him. His state of mind is summed up in these few lines:

I sense at hand a double death:
My spirit worn, my parting word is near;
Of the one I am certain, while the other threatens.

He worked on his *Universal Judgment*, commissioned by Pope Paul III Farnese, for a total of eight years, in which are to be seen « angels between earth and heaven and also evil, lustful, arrogant spirits, dark Hell and the Son of God surrounded by them all ».

Pope Paul III felt the time had come when Michelangelo should be rewarded for his toil, and, in a papal brief dated September 10, 1535, accordingly decreed that the « superb architect, sculptor and painter of the Apostolic Palace be aggregated to the family of the Holy Father with full honours ». He also awarded him an annual income *in perpetuum* of one thousand two hundred gold scudi for his work on the *Universal Judgment*.

Michelangelo had received from life all that is of most worth, namely, glory, sorrow, love, the agony of creation and faith in God. But he was by no means happy. His *Moses* testifies to his greatness, though in spite of this he lacked warmth and affection from without, and only in noble-minded, deserving persons was he able to place his unswerving trust and friendship, and in truth these persons numbered but few. Among the latter, he was closely attached to Vittoria Colonna, Marquise of Pescara; Urbino, his servant; Tommaso del Cavaliere; and a few others. Life was slipping from his grasp, his vital forces were on the wane, though his relatives kept watch over him; Florence was far away and the Pope continually pressed him to complete the *Cupola* of St. Peter's and to decorate with frescoes the Pauline Chapel. Yet Pope Julius III was a man of mediocre qualities who failed to understand him, ever wanting him at his side, though « embalmed ». In due course Michelangelo shunned the company of his fellow men, considering them to be liars and cheats who « wallow in the mire of sewers ».

Among so much sorrow, many happy, amusing details are to be found in the life of the great artist that render him all the more lovable. It is often said that he took no care of his person and in what he wore, that food meant nothing to him. Yet this is not altogether true. In his old age he enjoyed the pleasures of the table and on occasions was by no means impartial to good wine. He once wrote to his nephew, Lionardo: « I would rather have two flasks of Trebbiano (wine) than eight shirts ». He was fond of cheese made with fresh March milk, black and white chick-peas, beans, peas and apples. He exulted at the news announcing the birth of nephews and nieces, though he feared the « lunacy » of women, for women, to use his own words, were « always out to dominate ». Though he owned property both in town and country, he lamented at the fact that his brother, Sigismondo, toiled as a peasant and « lived among oxen ». As an old man he liked to bestow dowries on girls about to be married and give alms to the poor, though he was against the latter's knowing who had given the money.

He often toyed with the idea of taking a well-earned holiday. Yet his urge to travel could hardly have been deep-rooted, as on more than one occasion he changed his mind and returned home soon after starting out.

Little inclined to allow himself to be cheated, he always scrupulously administered his substance. With great filial love he once wrote thus to his father: « If I have put up with dire cicumstances and suffered their consequences. I have done so on your behalf. Whenever I have been able to, I have always done good. There is a matter that presses me, namely, that I must ask you forgiveness, for whatever may happen, I am still your son ». To his brother, Sigismondo, he instead dispatched a hard, unrelenting letter: « I no longer like you. I am now certain you are not my brother, because if you were, you would not threaten my father. Nay, you are brutish, and henceforward I shall treat you as a brute. May it be clear to you that whoever threatens or vexes his own father is destined to pay for his errors with his life. You undo in an hour what has laboriously taken me years to put together — I swear it, on the body of Christ! I am ready to destoy ten thousand of your likes should the need ever arise »! His nephew, Lionardo, often had to put up with Michelangelo's uncontrollable outbursts of anger, and the latter, having received from the former the gift of a few shirts, replied: « Your three shirts have arrived. I am very surprised you sent them to me, because so large are they in size that no man here is peasant enough to wear them ». At a later date he wrote to the same nephew: « I have been ill recently, and the scope of your visit was to see whether I should die and leave you anything. May God be with you, only from now on visit me no more and refrain from writing ».

Towards the beginning of February, 1564, Michelangelo, now being aged eighty-nine years, began to feel unwell; but obstinate as he was, he insisted on continuing with his back-breaking toil, giving himself wholly, as was his custom, to his sculpture and to superintending his labourers intent on building the Cupola of St. Peter's. In spite of the fact that it was raining heavily in those days, he was found out in the open by his beloved pupil, Tiberio Calcagni. When the latter protested at his state, Michelangelo replied drily: « I am ever restless and shall never find peace anywhere ». Some days later his strength appeared to be giving out and he was beset by a sense of profound sleepiness, though he still insisted on going out to work. But it was of no avail: worn out and greatly weakened, he was carried back home. He asked to be allowed to sit on chair by the fire, rather than lie in bed, as lying down made him impatient. The physicians Feder-

igo Donati and Gherardo Fedelissimi da Pistoia were called in. On their orders, he was put to bed and nursed by Tommaso del Cavaliere, Daniele da Volterra, Antonio del Francese and Diomede Leoni. Turning to Daniele, he muttered feebly: « O, Daniello, I am done and finished; but I beg you, do not leave me ». His illness and suffering lasted five days: in the evening of February 18, he passed away, sighing: « I hereby consign my soul to God, my body to the earth and my belongings to my nearest kin ».

Following his death, numerous sketches, drawings and unfinished sculptures, among them the *Rondanini Pietà*, were found in his house.

Thus the great artist departed this life, his fine, powerful hands finally finding eternal rest after long years of unflagging labour; perhaps at the moment of passing away his thoughts alighted on what he had once written:

> *The span of life has run its course,*
> *By stormy sea and fragile boat,*
> *To the common port;*
> *To enter which one must transcend*
> *The whys and wherefores of all work*
> *Both bad and good alike.*

The funeral ceremony in Rome cost forty-five scudi, while the waxed cloth to cover the coffin cost two and a half, reaching Giorgio Vasari on March 11. Twenty-five days had passed since Michelangelo's death, yet his body was found to be as fresh as it was the day he died, the expression on his face so serene and composed that it seemed he lay resting « in sweet, peaceful sleep ». In place of a shroud, he was dressed in green velvet, his feet being shod with slippers.

The coffin containing the mortal remains was transferred to Florence and placed on view in the Chapel of the Company of the Assumption, in the Church of San Pier Maggiore. The following day, Sunday, all the artists in Florence gathered together outside the church at dusk, and then entered to pay him homage, their heads uncovered. They found the coffin draped with a velvet cloth embroidered with gold, the whole surmounted by a crucifix. Having carried the coffin from the church, the younger among the artists took turns to bear it on their shoulders, while their older colleagues walked in file behind them holding torches, followed by a large crowd of people. From the Church of San Piero Maggiore the procession wound its way to Santa Croce, where the coffin was opened and placed in the repository near the altar of the Cavalcanti Chapel. On July 4, the solemn obsequies were held in the Church of San Lorenzo, in the presence of the Grand Duke Cosimo I. The funeral oration was declaimed, amid the general emotion of all those present, by Messer Benedetto Varchi, the great orator. That order should be maintained and the procession allowed to pass unhindered through the pressing crowds, the halberdiers of the Gran Duke

had to be called in. It is interesting to note that Benvenuto Cellini was absent from the ceremony.

In the 18th century Michelangelo's tomb in Santa Croce was first opened and his body found to be almost intact. In September, 1857, it was again opened, though this time the flesh of his body was all but reduced to dust; yet the « skeleton was still preserved in its entirety, except for the bones of the face and those in the fore part of the skull ». Round the head were found « several bay leaves and a mass of tangled coloured threads — perhaps of the hood — which, to the touch, crumbled to dust ». In his work, Michelangelo was severe with himself, vigorously discarding all that is cheap and second-rate in art. In his paintings he was not lavish and spared his colours, though taken as a whole, they are always complete in themselves and full of movement. He drove himself with furious impetus right to the end of his long life, and by doing so, attained the uppermost summit of sculpture, painting and architecture. Michelangelo is alone in his greatness and will always be so, a shining example of genius that belongs to the entire world.

AUTOGRAPH LETTER OF MICHELANGELO

11

1. - THE NEW SACRISTY

Six months after the death of Pope Julius II on March 15, 1513, Cardinal Giovanni dei Medici was raised to the papal throne. Carefree, and easy-going by nature, he assumed the high-sounding name of Leone X, and at the mere age of thirty-seven found the great responsibility of guiding the destiny of the Church, already shaken by the mighty voice of Martin Luther, cast upon his shoulders. Born in 1475, the same year as Michelangelo, as a child he had lived, studied and played with the future sculptor in the Medici Palace, in Via Larga, under the vigilant eyes of his beloved father, Lorenzo the Magnificent.

His election to the Papacy was well received by most people, especially by artists and men of letters, who were confident that the young Pope would follow in the steps of his illustrious family, renowned for its generosity as patrons of the arts.

Once all the pomp and ceremony of his coronation was over, Pope Leone X summoned his childhood companion to Rome and entrusted him with the drawing up of plans for the façade of the Church of San Lorenzo. Shortly afterwards, he went even further and commisioned the great sculptor, now turned architect, to plan a sepulchral chapel, in the vicinity of the Church, fit to receive the mortal remains of various members of his family.

Not being in a position to disobey the Pope, a friend and fellow Florentine to boot, Michelangelo with heavy heart was forced to take to Rome his sketches and drawings, prepared with great care for the façade as yet unbuilt, which so greatly pleased Leone X that he forbade Michelangelo to continue working on the tomb of his predecessor, Pope Julius II.

Michelangelo was thus obliged to submit himself to the Pope's will, and because of his honest, proud nature little given to servility, returned to Florence sad and embittered, yet fully determined to put his ability in the field of architecture to the test. It is interesting to note that hitherto Michelangelo had always considered architecture a secondary art, nurturing little enthusiasm for it.

However, though tired and dissatisfied, Michelangelo set immediately to work, his uppermost thought being that of honouring his promise to the Pope, and for well nigh three years he toiled at gathering together sufficient marble for the façade and at perfectioning his initial plans. Yet no sooner had he begun the actual work of building the façade than the Pope, in a brief dated March 12, 1520, and for reasons as yet unknown, freed Michelangelo from all obligations in connection with its construction.

Pope Leone X, after a reign lasting eight short years, died on December 1, 1521, having failed through his own fault to obtain from his friend both the façade and sepulchral chapel, at one time so greatly desired.

That Michelangelo fully intended satisfying the wishes of Pope Leone X is proved by the following passage taken from a letter written by the sculptor on May 2, 1517, to Domenico Boninsegni: « I feel sufficiently confident as to my ability to build the façade of San Lorenzo that both the architecture and sculpture therein contained might became the mirror of all Italy ».

Extant drawings of the façade, as well as the wooden model made of it by Baccio d'Agnolo, clearly demonstrate the extent to which Michelangelo in his capacity as architect tends to a typical sculptural plasticity of form, however lacking in boldness and genial impulse, later to be the predominant factor in the New Sacristy. The foregoing short premise dealing with the plans for the façade of San Lorenzo is essential for whoever intends studying and fully appreciating a second masterpiece by the hand of Michelangelo, namely, the New Sacristy, in turn linked for obvious reasons — chronological, historical and artistic — to the above plans.

Following the death of Pope Hadrian VI, Flemish by birth, a mere thirteen months after being raised to the papal throne, his place was taken by another Medici Pope, namely, Clement VII, son

of Giuliano dei Medici killed during the Pazzi Conspiracy in 1478.

In due course, Clement VII, in a further papal bull, again authorized Michelangelo to build the New Sacristy.

The scope of the New Sacristy was that of a family sepulchral chapel fit to contain the mortal remains of several of the Pope's relatives, namely, those of his uncle, Lorenzo the Magnificent; of his father, Giuliano; of his cousin, Giuliano, Duke of Nemours; and finally of his second cousin, Lorenzo, Duke of Urbino.

Not content with this, Clement VII later toyed with the idea of commissioning Michelangelo to design a further two tombs, to be placed in the centre of the Chapel, that is, one for himself and one for his late cousin, Pope Leone X.

It is interesting to note that Pope Clement VII, in spite of his ambiguousness in the field of politics and the difficulty in getting a clear picture of his character on account of his numerous psychological failings, nevertheless cherished a profound affection for Michelangelo, fully aware of his qualities both as a man and artist, and because of this was able to submit his will to that of the sculptor with tact, kindness and humility.

Proof of the sincerity of his sentiments is given in the following letter from the Pope to Michelangelo: « As you are well aware, Popes do not live to a ripe old age; and because of this, we could not wish more than to see the Chapel completed — ar at least in the process of being completed — together with the tombs of our relatives and also the Library. In view of this, we exhort you to proceed with the work in hand, and in the meanwhile we will be patient (as you once had occasion to request us), praying to God that He might instil you with energy and a good heart to help you in your task. And do not doubt that further commissions and prizes in the form of money will come your way as long as we are alive. And to conclude, may the blessing of both God and ourselves be upon you ».

The Pope granted Michelangelo the right to build the Chapel as he pleased and took pains never to force him to fulfil absurd or impossible requests, well aware that he had entrusted the task to an artist by now renowned throughout Italy and the entire civilized world. And in proof of his benevolence, he awarded Michelangelo a monthly salary of fifty gold ducats, to be increased should the latter ever request it.

And so Michelangelo, finding himself in a position of complete freedom to act as he pleased, was able to fully dedicate himself, as he described it, to the construction of stupendous « architectural poetry », rich in powerful, refined effects. With untold skill and inspiration, Michelangelo thus marked the boundaries of the Florentine Renaissance in a manner never seen before or since. In building the Chapel, he made use of the Corinthian order of architecture, to be found in the divisions of the columns placed one upon the other, and discarded the Doric order, in spite of the fact that the latter is often considered more suited to the construction of funeral monuments and architecture, and not unjustly so. In truth, Michelangelo was much averse to copying the ideas of others, though in this case he bent traditional precepts to his own particular interpretation, however odd, of classical rules. Giorgio Vasari was well aware of this when, referring to Michelangelo's imitators, he wrote thus: « The licence shown by Michelangelo has greatly encouraged all those who have taken it upon themselves to imitate him, with the result that their ornamentation betrays a whole fantastic range of images, conceived in grotesque fashion rather than by rule or reason ».

If certain incongruities of style committed here by Michelangelo are overlooked, the New Sacristy may be compared in beauty of architecture and finish to the Old Sacristy, designed and built by Filippo Brunelleschi, that is, to the extent to which the two edifices have points in common.

In building the Chapel, Michelangelo was clearly out to obtain a three-dimensional effect, thus breathing life into the general mass, the various elements of which, excluding the statues, are set off against the bare walls in vivid contrast, namely, by the grey of the stone-work against the white of the plastered background.

The edges of the cornices are both sharp and jutting, and whereas the absence of concave niches and alcoves is marked, rectangular forms and shallow spaces abound: of illogical concept, the latter are nevertheless acceptable once in a while, especially if designed by one as great as Michelangelo.

Work on the Chapel was commenced in March, 1521, and all but finished by the beginning of 1524, when the lantern was added to the small cupola. Yet Michelangelo, though he had nearly completed the statues, was obliged to go to Rome, with the result that the Grand Duke Cosimo I had no other choice than to entrust the completion of the interrupted work to Vasari and Ammannati, who, instead of modifying the original plans, merely limited themselves to arranging the layout of the Chapel as it is seen today. This was due to the fact that Michelangelo before his death burnt the bulk of his designs for the New Sacristy, thus making it impossible to know his true intentions as regards its final arrangement.

The concept uppermost in Michelangelo's mind while building the New Sacristy was that of death, not only in connection with the various members of the Medici family whom he immortalized in marble, but also in every one of us. His thoughts on this subject are borne out by the Holy Scriptures, of which he was a profound judge.

Vanity of vanities; all is vanity.

(Eccl. I)

On entering the Chapel and facing the altar, the sightseer will find the tomb of Lorenzo, Duke of Urbino, immediately to his left, namely, directly opposite that of Giuliano, Duke of Nemours, on the right.

Lorenzo, Duke of Urbino, was born to Piètro and Alfonsina Orsini on September 2, 1492, the same year in which his grandfather, Lorenzo the Magnificent, died. Though as a young man he was not excessively gifted, at the age of nineteen he was already actively engaged in the political life of the time, taking care, however, not to neglect the gallantries and amusements then in vogue. In 1513 he came to Florence to take up office as ruler of the state and outlying region, and in this capacity, at least at the outset, governed Tuscany with « prudence and diligence ». Yet Pope Leone X mas not altogether convinced of his abilities as a statesman when he wrote that « I created a Captain who has no experience whatever and who fills the post of practical men. Should difficulties make themselves manifest, I am unaware as to how he will ever be able to resolve them ». In fact, the Duke, who considered himself « young and in flesh », preferred the graces of beautiful women such as Orsola, Teresa da Savorgnano, Beatrice da Ferrara and others to the grave burdens of office. And so, with the passing of the years, and perhaps missing the guiding hand of the Pope and his family, what few qualities the Duke once had were now dissipated forever. In due course, he took up his « baton of command » in the league against Francis I of France, leading « the militia of the people of Florence », though failed to put in an appearance in any action worthy of mention. Routed by the Swiss and French at the Battle of Marignano on September 13, 1515, his first thought was to surrender his army and seek peace terms with such speed that his mother, Alfonsina Orsini, was put to shame by his unmanly behaviour. In 1518 he married Madeleine de la Tour, daughter of Jean, Comte de Auvergne, and Catherine Bourbon de Vendôme, though the union, celebrated in Paris, rather than based on reciprocal love, was one of convenience (*mariage de convenance*), in which family interests had the upper hand.

By nature, Lorenzo, the son of Piero, was moody and presumptuous, though Marino Giorgi, praising him, wrote thus: « He is astute and well-suited to action, not to the extent that Valentino is, but almost ». Though traditon makes him out to be competent and pleasant by nature at the beginning of his carrer, Cambi the historian, as early as 1514, judges him most severely: «Giuliano de' Medici and Lorenzo, his nephew, governed Florence with a rod of iron, as if they were lords and gentlemen ». Yet aided and abetted by the members of his court, by the Pope, his mother and others, he was able, to quote Capponi, « to oppress by the authority of false votes, to overcome by gentle seduction, to bribe with money and soften with the promise of easy living, all those who loved liberty, and thus made the City, hitherto content to have Lorenzo as its head, sooner tolerate Alessandro ». In addition to this, Bartolommeo Cerretani, contemporary to Lorenzo, leaves a gloomy picture of his reign: « The governing bodies in a state of total disorder and magistrates without pity, ever ready to obey the wishes of the Duke and his mother at the slightest heed. Arms were carried on all occasions, even when not called for: the common citizen was ever at the mercy of the Duke's veteran bodyguard of lancers and a disorganized mass of villainous young Florentines ». In 1516, Niccolò Machiavelli dedicated his political treatise, *The Prince*, to Lorenzo, certainly a move

full of significance, when one considers the great statesman's thoughts regarding rulers of states: « A prudent man cannot and must not observe the faith, when such observance turns against him, and when the reasons for its having been promised no longer exist ».

He thus identifies Lorenzo, and imaginatively so, with the « prince » destined to bring peace to his country, torn and divided by civil war.

Lorenzo had little time for the arts, especially music, which he found abominable, far preferring « the hounds of Magistro Juliano, the hawks of Monsignor Cibo, and the gay company of gentlewomen ». He found studying methodically irksome and kept well clear of meetings between artists and men of letters. In spite of this, Raphael was commissioned by him to paint a canvas of the Madonna with St. Michael, to be presented to the King of France. He lived to the age of twentyseven and died without attaining full maturity. He was weak of will and greatly given to sensual pleasures. As to his weakness, Gaetano Pieraccini has this to say of him: « He was totally deficient in spirituality, and not without reason was called by some "Lorenzuolo", little, insignificant Lorenzo ».

As to his appearance, the following account is given of him: « He was of medium height, strong and vigorous in body, with a full, though pale, face and chestnut hair. He carried himself in a dignified manner, and his eyes, when blazing with anger, filled one with fear ». Raphael painted his portrait in 1518; as to its fate, both Cavalcaselle and Crowe place it in the year 1891 as being in the possession of one Mr. Hollingsworth, of Colworth, England. On the other hand, the portrait in the Uffizi Gallery, following research carried out by Professor Poggi, is attributed to Alessandro del Barbiere.

Lorenzo died on May 4, 1519, of syphilis and tuberculosis of the lung and intestines, shortly after his wife, Madeleine, who died of puerperal fever, having given birth to a daughter, Catherine, later to become Queen of France.

The composition of the funeral monument as conceived by Michelángelo is, from an architectural

18

4

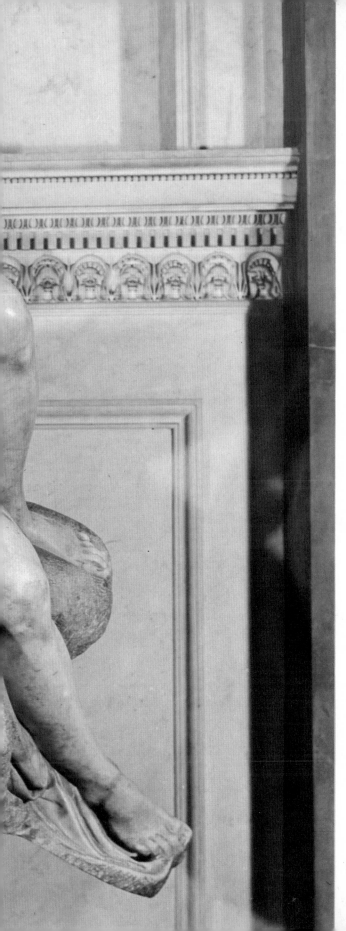

and sculptural aspect, clearly one of perfect unity. The tomb containing the remains of the Duke, together with the recumbent figures representing *Dawn* and *Twilight*, and also the likeness of him incorporated in the statue contained in the rectangular niche, is of surpassing beauty. The latter statue of the Duke, still known as *il Pensieroso*, the « Thinker », dominates the group, his face being overshadowed by the helmet, while those of *Dawn* and *Twilight* lie on their beds of stone as if contemplating eternal death. Taking into consideration the austere nature of Michelangelo, one is at a loss to understand why he created a work of such beauty to honour the memory of one so worthless. The features of the Thinker in no way resemble those of Lorenzo di Urbino. Rather Michelangelo has depicted a mythical hero whose deeply tormented gaze betrays sad, grave thoughts that are also of despair, in this case brought about by the rapid passage of time which, with inexorable stride, carries away all before it and reduces man to impalpable dust.

From an early pen-and-ink sketch, today in the British Museum, it is clear just how Michelangelo originally intended to arrange the statues and tombs in the Chapel. In fact, the statues are shown as being joined together, while the tombs rest on plinths raised from the ground and supported, in keeping with artistic trends of the Renaissance, by four carved lion's paws. The details of certain friezes recall the attic of the New Sacristy as it is today. In a second sketch, also in the British Museum, the original plan is slightly modified and simplified, while the masses are perhaps more severe in outline. The statues, still recumbent, face each other and are turned towards the central axis of the tomb. Other sketches were also prepared by Michelangelo, for instance those at Oxford, the Louvre and elsewhere, all of which go to show just how much Michelangelo must have pondered over his plans prior to hitting on the final solution. Yet, examining more closely the tomb of the Duke Lorenzo, one is still perplexed as to just what were Michelangelo's real intentions regarding his work. Giovanni Duprè had this to say on the matter when, in 1875, he wrote: « For my part, leaving others to judge for

7

themselves, I can only point out that the generation able to penetrate into the depths of Michelangelo's mind perhaps still belongs to the future. Each one of us can only do what his capabilities allow him to do, casting his gaze as far as it will take him. Michelangelo cast his into the regions of eternal light. His soul is reborn each day for whoever has in him a quality that is unaware of the meaning of death, namely, the divine spark that unites beauty with good ».

Apart from the above, another point of interest that still considerably perplexes art critics is the unifished state of the statue symbolzing *Twilight* Much has been written and said in this respect, especially in regard to other works of Michelangelo, though in the case of *Twilight*, exhaustive, acceptable explanations are still wanting. Lack of time would be a plausible enough answer to the question. That Michelangelo was hard pressed for time is certainly true, though it still cannot be denied that he was unable to finish the head of *Twilight*, when one considers that he was able to complete in a superb manner the accompanying statue of *Dawn*. Perhaps he deemed it just to finish the latter, essentially a womanly figure, while leaving some parts of *Twilight* merely roughed out, thus accentuating its inherent virility. Michelangelo was thus, on more than one occasion in his art, an innovator without equal, and the liberty he often took when carving his statues cannot but draw one closer to him. Not without reason did a friend and pupil say of him: « Michelangelo was the most modern among the moderns ».

8. - TOMB OF GIULIANO, DUKE OF NEMOURS (*New Sacristy*)

9. - STATUE OF NIGHT
10. - STATUE OF DAY
11. - DETAIL OF THE STATUE OF NIGHT
12. - DETAIL OF THE STATUE OF DAY
13. - STATUE OF GIULIANO

The tomb of Giuliano, Duke of Nemours, stands to the right of the altar, opposite that of Lorenzo, Duke of Urbino. The two figures lying on it are symbolical, the man representing *Day* and the woman *Night*, while above is the statue of Duke Giuliano of Nemours (1479-1516), son of Lorenzo the Magnificent and Clarice Orsini. Michelangelo carved him in a sitting position, clasping the « baton of command », in this case that of Captain of the Church Militia. The thought underlying the creation of these two tombs seems to be that Time — represented by the four recumbent figures — destroys the Action and Thought of men as represented in the figures of the two princes.

While Michelangelo was working on the statues, Giovanni, the son of Carlo Strozzi, having seen one of them already completed, sent the sculptor the following lines:

Night whom you see in such sweet attitude sleep
Was carved by an Angel from this stone;
And because it sleeps, has life.
O unbeliever, wake it, and hear it speak!

Michelangelo wasted no time and his answer was brief and somewhat bitter:

Dear to me is sleep, and more so to be of stone,
'Cause evil and shame live after man;
Not to see and feel is my fortune;
So do not wake me, nay, speak low!

What other choice was left to Michelangelo, having been forced much against his will to glorify in marble two worthless princes? On the one hand, Lorenzo of Urbino, by nature lazy, fainthearted and morally corrupt; and, on the other, Giuliano of Nemours, sickly, sensitive and much given to the pleasures of the flesh. As a way out

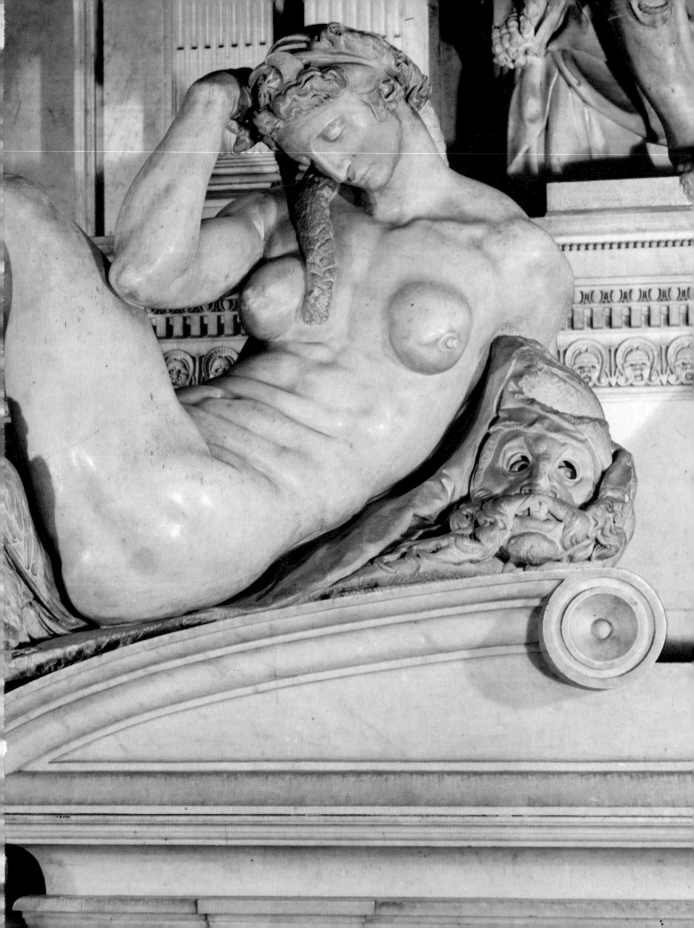

of his dilemma, Michelangelo, who was very familiar with the works of Dante, perhaps bore in mind the following lines from the Divine Comedy when carving the statues of Day and Night:

Your renown
Is as the herb, whose hue doth come and go;
And his might withers it, by whom it sprang
Crude from the lap of earth.

In spite of Michelangelo's reluctance to carve the various statues in the Chapel, those of *Day* and *Night* more than gratify the expectations of the art-lover, proving once more the unparalleled greatness of the sculptor's art. If, on the other hand, criticism is to be raised, it may be directed only on the tomb, which, in respect of the two recumbent figures, is a shade on the small side. However, this is no fault of Michelangelo, but rather of his pupils, who, after their master had moved to Rome, failed to correctly interpret his drawings.

Turning to Giuliano himself, it is interesting to note that the likeness incorporated into his statue by Michelangelo in no way corresponds to the descriptions left by historians of the time. Michelangelo was well aware of this discrepancy and to those who asked him the reason for it, he was wont to reply that a mere two centuries later no one would notice that anything was amiss. Yet if the effeminate features of the face do not resemble Giuliano physically, they at least tie up with with his character. To better understand Michelangelo's subtle interpretation of his subject's psychological make-up, it is of interest to note what several persons contemporary to Giuliano have to say in this respect. For example, Matteo Franco, his tutor, has left this curious description of his ward as a child: « Giuliano is fresh as a rose, clear as a mirror, contemplative by nature,

and has fine eyes ». As a youth he was a weakling and also in manhood. In proof of this, another contemporary describes him thus: « He was tall and slender, with long arms and blue eyes... of weak constitution ». He had his portrait painted by Raphael; according to some, the painting is to be found in Berlin, while others place it in New York.

In the summer of 1515, the illness from which Giuliano was soon to die first made itself manifest. The month of his death is given as February, 1516, and the following account describes the circumstances in which he passed away: « As the days went by, he grew steadily worse. Having out of weariness had himself carried to the Badia at Fiesole (where lived Filiberta, his woman, who lived a pious existence), he there died of consumption a few days later ».

During his lifetime he was fond of music and poetry which he wrote. Fatini, the most complete biographer of Giuliano, has this to say: « If, in spite of his having made a name for himself as a poet — in his capacity as a modest composer of rhymes, rather than as a philisopher — he is to be left out of the annals of the Medici family, he at least should be included in the historical events of the 16th century ». He counted among his friends Leonardo da Vinci, Andrea del Sarto and Lodovico Ariosto. Brantôme called him « la fleur de toute chevalerie », while others mention that « for his men- and gentlemen-at-arms he spent a mint of money », and also that, at the time of his death, he left « infinite debts, being very liberal ». If he never shone in the field of politics, he at least left a good account of himself. In fact, the best words — three in number — ever said of Giuliano, Duke of Nemours, are to be found in the report drawn up by Marino Giorgi on March 17, 1517, and dispatched to the Republic of Venice: « He was an honest man ».

14. - TOMB OF LORENZO THE MAGNIFICENT AND HIS BROTHER, GIULIANO DEI MEDICI (*New Sacristy*)

15. - DETAIL OF THE STATUE OF THE MADONNA

Standing above the centre of the long marble tomb containing the mortal remains of Lorenzo the Magnificent and his brother, Giuliano dei Medici, is a fine Madonna and Child, also carved by Michelangelo, with on either side the statues of SS. Cosmas and Damian, respectively the work of his pupils Raffaello da Montelupo and Giovannangelo da Montorsoli.

The above Madonna, together with the one included in the Pietà at St. Peter's, Rome, may well be considered the finest ever carved by Michelangelo. Through unfinished, the face of the Virgin Mary wears an expression of spiritual sweetness without equal, and is fashioned with rare delicacy that is unusual in Michelangelo, if one is to consider his customary bold, vigorous manner in sculpture.

The statue of St. Cosmas is the fruit of a close collaboration between Michelangelo and his pupil, Raffaello da Montelupo, the former having fashioned for the latter a preliminary model in clay of the Saint's head and arms.

Fra Giovannangelo dei Servi della Nunziata da Montorsoli (1507-1563), sculptor and architect, pupil of Michelangelo. Among his works are the fountain of Neptune and Orion at Messina, the tomb of Sannazzaro at Naples, the tomb of Andrea Doria at Genoa, and the bust of Tommaso Cavalcanti in the Church of Santo Spirito, Florence.

16. - THE LAURENTIAN, OR MEDICI, LIBRARY
(*Biblioteca Medicea Laurenziana*)

Michelangelo began working on his plans for the Library in 1524, having duly been commissioned by Pope Clement VII dei Medici. The scope of the Library was to hold priceless codices and manuscripts formerly in the possession of Cosimo the Elder and Lorenzo the Magnificent. However, work of building the edifice was temporarily suspended following the death of Pope Clement VII, though was later completed under the auspices of the Grand Duke Cosimo I, who opened the Library to the public in 1571.

By the hand of Michelangelo is the entrance-hall together with its niches, in which various statues symbolizing the arts and sciences were to have been placed. The Reading Room, as well as the bookcases, shelving and ornamentation, is also the work of Michelangelo. At a later date, Michelangelo, being absent in Rome and thus unable to continue superintending the work of building, duly instructed Giorgio Vasari by letter as to how to erect the staircase leading to the Library. « With regard to the staircase », he wrote, « believe me, I should not hesitate to explain it to you in detail, if I could but remember with exactness how I originally planned it. Yet I recall, as in a dream, a certain staircase, though I have good reason to believe it is not the one I formerly had in mind, in that it is awkward and anything but logical. Nevertheless, however it may be, here is a description of it... ». He then proceeds to describe the strange arrangement of ovoid steps and how they should be built, concluding thus: « What I have described above will no doubt make you laugh, though I feel sure you will agree there is method in my madness ». Yet the fact that Michelangelo sent Ammannati a wooden model of the stairs three years later leads one to think that the building of the staircase was not carried out by Vasari, as is generally supposed, but rather by Ammannati. It was Michelangelo's wish that the stairs should be made of wood; however, the Grand Duke Cosimo thought otherwise, and though praising the wooden model, ordered them to be built of stone.

17 - 18. - PIETÀ, OR DEPOSITION FROM THE CROSS
(*Duomo or Cathedral of Santa Maria del Fiore*)

This superb group, depicting the Deposition from the Cross, was carved by Michelangelo between 1545 and 1550, after he had already finished decorating the Pauline Chapel with frescoes. The work, profound in dramatic sense, was executed at the height of his artistic maturity, and is of such force as to be equal in all respect to the other three similar groups carved at different periods of his life.

The greatness of Michelangelo's work is revealed to the full in all its severity, at once rugged and powerful. The body of Christ devoid of life, supported by the Virgin Mary, dominates the other figures. To the left, Mary Magdalene, better finished though less grandiose than the Virgin Mary, is inserted into the group as a mere supporting element, thus rounding off the whole. Above them, the sad expression of his face hidden in the shadow of his hood, appears Nicodemus, who, almost embracing the Mother and her Son, is united to them in his immense grief.

It is believed that Michelangelo carved the Deposition from a block of marble formely incorporated in an ancient Roman temple, namely, from a capital surmounting one of the eight massive columns in Vespasian's Temple of Peace. However, the block in question was very hard and full of flaws, with the result that it caused Michelangelo considerable trouble, and this also goes to explain why the work was left unfinished. It is cracked in numerous places, perhaps due to having been dropped while being moved from Rome to Florence. According to Vasari, the group was first at the Villa di Monte Cavallo, belonging to Pierantonio Bandini, the son of Francesco, and the exact date of its transfer to Florence is not known. Having been brought to the latter city, it lay for some years in the marble storeyard in which material was kept for the building of the New Sacristy, in the Church of San Lorenzo, until in 1722, the Grand Duke Cosimo III had it placed in the Cathedral in the position it still occupies today.

If we are to believe Vasari, it was Michelangelo himself who damaged his own masterpiece. In support of this, Vasari has written: « Having reasoned at length, he asked him why he had broken it, thus spoiling the fruit of so much wondrous labour; to which he replied that it was the importunity of Urbino, his servant, who daily urged him to finish it; and that, among other things, a piece of the Madonna's elbow had been broken off, and also prior to this, he had grown to hate the very sight of the group and had much trouble in the carving of a single hair; so much so that he lost his patience and snapped off the latter and would have smashed the whole group had not Antonio del Francese, his servant, begged Michelangelo to give him the group as it was. Whereupon Tiberio Calcagni (his favourite pupil) having heard this, spoke of the matter to Bandino (Francesco Bandini, friend to Michelangelo), who was anxious to have something by the hand of Michelangelo. Following which, Bandino made Tiberio promise to pay Antonio two hundred gold scudi, and then asked Michelangelo that should he so wish, Tiberio would finish the group with the help of models on behalf of Bandino, with the result that so much labour would not be wasted in vain. Michelangelo was pleased by his suggestion and made them a present of it. The group was immediately taken away by Tiberio, who set to work on it, though was left unfinished on account of the deaths of Bandino, Michelangelo and Tiberio ».

That Michelangelo had originally destined the work to adorn his tomb is not proved by any extant documents. On the other hand, on observing the face of Nicodemus more closely, it will be noticed that his features, especially the flat nose, resemble those of Michelangelo. However, it is common knowledge that many artists, often quite unintentionally, are wont to portray themselves for various psychological reasons, not easily explained even today, in spite of the great progress made in objective and experimental psychology.

From a study of documents to be found in various Florentine archives, it results that on August 15, 1501, Michelangelo obtained from the Opera del Duomo (Cathedral Works Department) a block of white Carrara marble, from which he was to carve his statue of David.

In the contract drawn up between the sculptor and those who had commissioned the work, it was established that his monthly salary was to be six gold florins, and also that the statue was to be completed in its entirety two years from the date of being ordered.

However, matters turned out differently, and Michelangelo did not finish the statue in the two years allocated him: only on January 25, 1504, was he able to remove the scaffolding from around his colossus and show his astonished fellow citizens what was already a masterpiece.

The block of marble issued to the sculptor proved to be full of cracks and flaws, not only externally, but also internally. In addition, as early as 1464, Agostino di Duccio had attempted to carve a gigantic statue from the block in question, all but ruining it in the process; then at a loss as to what to do with it, he gave up the arduous task. And thus it fell to Michelangelo to make amends for the errors of his unfortunate predecessor.

The presence of so-called « foreign bodies », also defined in the language of sculptors as « emery streaks » or « chainlets », was already to be found in the interior of the block, which facilitate erosion and the appearance of fractures through a purely chemical process of disintegration.

In spite of the state in which Agostino had reduced the block of marble, Michelangelo was averse to refusing the commission, and thereby succeeded, to quote Vasari, « in resuscitating one who was already dead ».

As to the whereabouts of Michelangelo's studio, one P. Parenti has this to say in his *Storie Fiorentine* dated 1504: « In the Opera di Santa Maria del Fiore (where today stands the Cathedral Museum) was carved a colossal statue in white marble by Michelangelo Buonarroti, sculptor extraordinary; and it having been deliberated at length as to where the statue should be placed, it was finally decided *on the advice of the Master himself* that this should be Piazza della Signoria, where it was duly dragged by men with the aid of rollers, the task taking three days to complete ».

The above undertaking took place in April, and apart from Michelangelo himself, Leonardo da Vinci, Alessandro Botticelli, Pietro Perugino, as well as Giovanni the fife-player, father of Benvenuto Cellini, Gallieno the embroiderer and Messer Francesco, herald of the Signoria, were all consulted in turn as to where the statue should be placed. The Priors of Florence decreed that all those citizens in a position to do so should offer to help Michelangelo to the best of their ability during the said month of April, especially regarding the transport of the statue. In due course, the latter was secured and bolted in a stout wooden crate, which was then hoisted onto four rollers and dragged to Piazza della Signoria by forty men.

Once the statue had reached its destination, a plinth for it was commissioned by the Signoria from Simone del Pollaiolo called Cronaca and Antonio da San Gallo, while Michelangelo set about retouching his work, working from the head downwards.

While the sculptor was intent on adding his finishing touches, Pier Soderini, Gonfalonier of Florence, chanced to pass through the square. The latter, wishing to tell Michelangelo what he thought of the statue, called the sculptor's attention to David's nose. In his modest opinion, he said, David's nose was far too large for the gaunt face of the biblical hero who had slain Goliath. As was to be expected, Michelangelo was anything but convinced. And so in order to politely dispose of the good Gonfalonier, he resorted to the artful ruse recounted below by Vasari in his *Life of Michelangelo*:

« ... Thus to satisfy Soderini, Michelangelo climbed up the scaffolding; and swiftly taking hold of a chisel in his right hand and a little marble dust in his left, he pretended to lightly rub the offending nose, letting the dust fall to the ground. '' What do you think of it now ''? cried Miche-

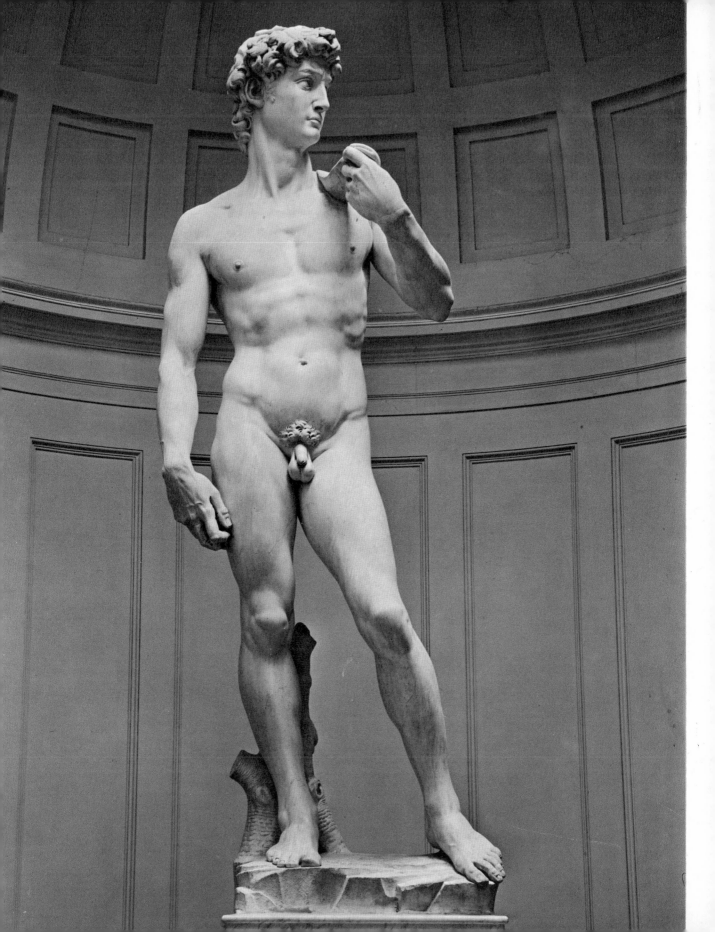

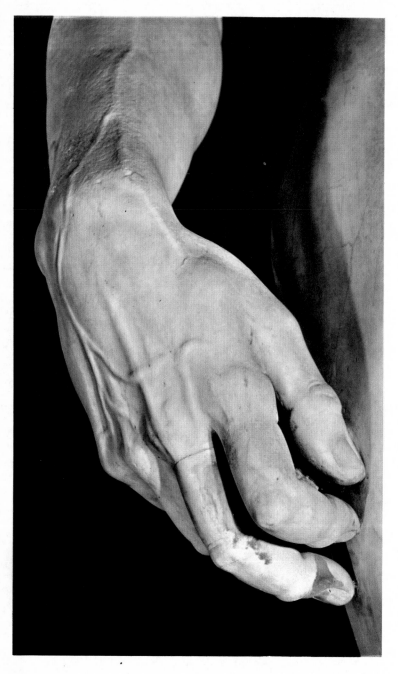

langelo. "Much better", replied Soderini, satisfied with the result. "You have indeed given it life".

During the rioting that took place at the time of the Medici family's expulsion from Florence in 1527, the left arm of David was smashed by a stone into three parts in the region of the pulse. However, the fragments were carefully gathered together by Cecchin Salviati and Giorgio Vasari — both boys at the time — and later repaired in 1543 by order of the Grand Duke Cosimo I.

In due course, the statue was removed from Piazza della Signoria on July 31, 1837, and four days later, on August 4, was already installed in the position in which it still stands today. The reason for its removal, apart from corrosion through exposure to the elements, was the discovery of a crack about a tenth of an inch in width running down the whole length of the statue, the consequences of which were particularly grave in the left foot. The height of the statue measures just over 13 feet.

Michelangelo depicts his biblical hero in the nude, ready to set upon Goliath and thus liberate his native land from the grips of her hated, tyrannical enemy. In his capacity as avenging angel guided by God, David expresses multiple moods: his face beneath his curly yet tempestuous locks is proud, while his threatening brow, furrowed with anger denotes unbending will; his penetrating gaze challenges and dominates the space immediately in front of it, as if measuring up the mortal blow, while the trembling nostrils breathe in the motionless air, prelude to the fight, and the parted lips seem about to shout a deafening war-cry. The body, of noble, masculine beauty, is slightly twisted and leans on the left leg. Its right counterpart is fully outstretched, the foot being placed forward as if reflecting the agility of the body poised ready to strike. The right arm hangs down one side, the powerful hand of which, with its tense, corded veins, holds the fatal stone in its hollow.

20

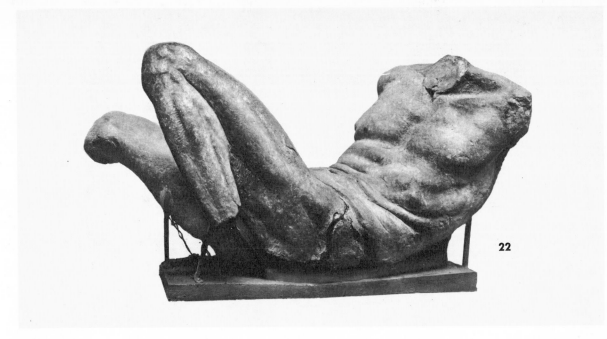

22

22. - TORSO OF FIUME (*Gallery of the Academy*)

When drawing up his plans for the New Sacristy, Michelangelo originally intended to place there more tombs and sculptures than are to be seen today, namely, several statues symbolizing Rivers, among them, the Arno, Tiber, Taro, Metaurus and Ticino. The latter were to have been placed on the floor of the Chapel, next to the plinths of the various tombs. With this in mind, Michelangelo fashioned a number of preliminary models in clay, without carving them later in marble, as was his wish. However, one of these models, truly a masterpiece, still exists today and is reproduced here.

23. - ST. MATTHEW (*Gallery of the Academy*)

On April 24, 1503, Michelangelo was commissioned by the Consuls of the Guild of Wool Merchants and the so-called Opera di Santa Maria del Fiore (Cathedral Works Department) to carve a series of twelve statues, among them that of St. Matthew, to replace the twelve Apostles painted by Bicci di Lorenzo in the Cathedral of Santa Maria del Fiore. He was allowed a period of twelve years to complete the sculptures, a monthly salary of two gold florins and a house in Borgo Pinti, in which to work unimpeded. In spite of the foregoing advantages set down in the clauses of the contract, Michelangelo was only able to commence carving the statue of St. Matthew.

The face of the Apostle, breaking free from the stony heart of the massive block, is barely visible, together with the powerful, twisted limbs of the great body, while the extent of the various planes rough-hewn by the sculptor throws into relief the mass as a whole.

The work, of great beauty even though unfinished, both teaches and proves to the art-lover the way in which figures are shaped from blocks of marble without their being irremediably marred.

In 1931 it was decided to transfer the statue from the Opera del Duomo to the Academy of Fine Arts, where it is now on view. The inscription on the plinth is by G. B. Niccolini.

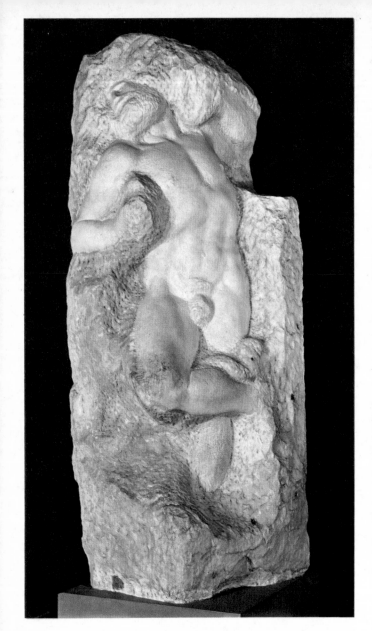

24 - 25 - 26 - 27. - THE PRISONERS *(Gallery of the Academy)*

The four so-called Prisoners which, though unfinished, constitute in themselves a masterpiece, were originally intended by Michelangelo for the tomb of Pope Julius II. At a later date they were presented by Lionardo Buonarroti, nephew of Michelangelo, to the Grand Duke Cosimo I dei Medici, who, devoid as he was of any feeling for things beautiful (at least in this case), had the statues placed in the artificial grotto made by Buontalenti in the Boboli Garden. Yet they were not destined to remain there forever and were eventually removed to the Gallery of the Academy in 1909.

The Prisoners, in an act of rebellion and anguish, crushed as they are by the immense weight of the marble, call to mind over the bridge of the centuries the tragic caryatids of Giovanni Pisano: one almost seems to hear their tragic cry of revolt,

that of beings without hope of salvation, in brief, giants of stone.

In 1505 Michelangelo was summoned to Rome by Pope Julius, who, for a payment of one hundred ducats, commissioned him to build a great tomb worthy of his name and standing, such as to excel in beauty, dimensions and abundance of statues any other sepulchre hitherto created. As was to be expected, the sculptor welcomed with enthusiasm the challenge of the bellicose Pope, and accordingly designed a massive sepulchre to be surmounted by as many as forty statues, without taking into account the bronze bas-reliefs that would have adorned the spaces between the figures of Prophets and Prisoners. As for Michelangelo's intentions regarding the tomb, he briefly sums them up in a letter to Sangallo as follows: « If the tomb is worth doing, it is worth doing well ». Contrary to expectation, the Pope did not keep his word, and thus began for Michelangelo the tragic sequence of events that was to plague him for the rest of his life.

A further two Prisoners are to be seen in the Museum of the Louvre, at Paris.

28 - 29. - THE PALESTRINA PIETÀ
(*Gallery of the Academy*)

The sculpture, little known until about thirty years ago, was formerly to be found in the village of Palestrina, not far from Rome, where it stood in a chapel consecrated to St. Rosalie belonging to the Barberini family. It was purchased by the State in 1939 and presented to the City of Florence, where it may now be seen in the Gallery of the Academy. The work was carved by Michelangelo late in life, together with the so-called *Rondanini Pietà,* formerly in the Palazzo Sanseverino-Vimercati, overlooking the Corso in Rome, and now in Milan.

The work, long-neglected by tradition as to its sources during the centuries following its completion, was carved from a colossal fragment of a Roman temple dating from the Imperial era; in the corner-edge to the right of the block, an architectural motif, perhaps representing the egg-and-dart cyma or dentils of an acanthus leaf, is clearly visible.

To the onlooker the group — in turn freed of an ungraceful drape dating from the 17th century — calls to mind but a single name: that of Michelangelo. Only Michelangelo had it in him to conceive a work on so tragic and severe a scale as this. The body of Christ, borne by loving hands, is depicted being taken down from the cross, almost as if falling into the sepulchre. By now the Saviour is dead and only grief remains the lot of those who saw his bloodstained cross at Golgotha; His body is nothing but an empty shell devoid of life.

More than ever before Michelangelo, in the later Depositions, is absorbed by bodily death, a subject that fascinates him above all others, in that he feels death near at hand, ready to snatch him away, as is clear from the following lines:.

Our eyes once shone in every cavern,
Though now are hollow, dark and horrible,
Dragging behind them the light of time —
Shadows o'er the sun, smoke on the wind.

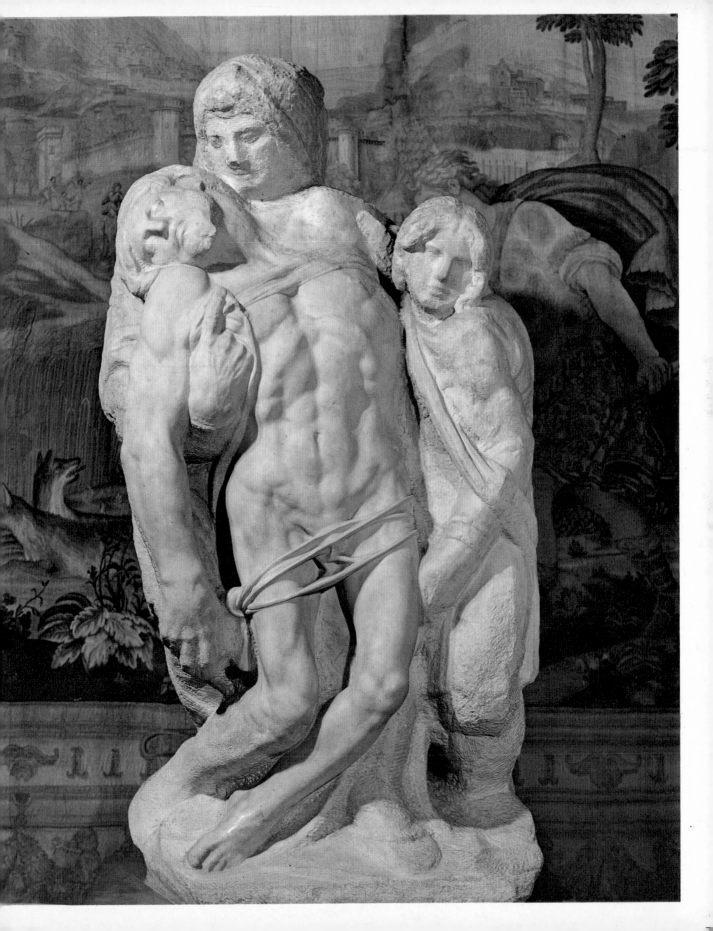

30. - HOLY FAMILY (*Uffizi Gallery*)

The *Holy Family*, also known as the Tondo Doni, is a circular painting on wood with a diameter of 3'8". Vasari describes it thus:

« Michelangelo painted a *tondo,* taking as his subject the Virgin Mary, on behalf of Angelo Doni, fellow citizen, friend and native of Florence, who was fond of beautiful things, both ancient and modern. He depicted the Virgin Mary in a kneeling position, with the Child Jesus in her arms, in the act of presenting Him to Joseph, who receives Him. It is clear from the tender gaze of the Mother of Christ bending over her Son that, radiant in her profound affection and marvellous sense of contentment, she is anxious to unite her joy with that of Joseph. The latter in turn makes as if to take the Child with an equal sense of love, tenderness and reverence, as is evident without studying too closely the expression of his face. Not content with this, Michelangelo, in order to heighten even further the greatness of his art, painted into the background of the work in question many nude figures, in a leaning, standing or sitting position, and with such diligence and cleanliness that, of all his paintings on wood, hitherto scarce as they are, this may be considered the finest and most finished ».

The work dates from either 1503 or 1505, and is Michelangelo's first known painting of importance, in which the inherent plasticity of the figures is clearly by the hand of a sculptor rather than of a painter. In fact, as to this plasticity of form, he wrote thus to Benedetto Varchi in 1549: « I feel that painting is better when it tends to be in relief, and likewise relief diminishes when it becomes a painting ».

The juxtaposition of colours, evenly balanced among themselves, lends to the whole an effective solemnity that blends easily with the complex twisting of the figures, to such an extent that it is almost a prelude to mannerism.

Michelangelo leaves nothing to narrative decorativism, but rather submits each element to the rigid laws of contrast between light and shadow, squeezing all his subjects into the narrow confines of the circular painting with the mathematical precision of a great artist able to resolve technical problems however difficult; and all but discarding preciosity in the use of colour, he obtains results that are both solemn and concise, discovering at the same time horizons untried by others, and thus attains conclusions rich in charm and strength. The fact that he has painted nude figures in the background is apt to cause surprise in the onlooker, though Michelangelo was by no means first in the field, having been preceded by Luca Signorelli. In support of this, a painting by the latter artist depicting — as in the case of Michelangelo — the Holy Family may be seen in the Uffizi Gallery. Bearing this in mind, it is likely that Michelangelo, returning to Florence from Rome, passed through Orvieto to see Luca Signorelli's frescoes of the Universal Judgment, thus finding many points in common between the art of Signorelli and his own, ever monumental and austere.

In the upper part of the gilded circular frame — contemporary to the painting itself and moreover a worthy complement — may be seen the Strozzi coat of arms, namely, three half moons, added there on the occasion of Maddalena Strozzi's marriage to Agnolo Doni, who presented the masterpiece to his bride.

From the smooth, accurate, clean manner in which the work is executed, and also from the uniform evenness, relative aridity of style and coldness of colour, it is generally thought that Michelangelo painted the Holy Fomily using the so-called *tempera,* or distemper, medium: a technique he preferred to all others, especially to painting with oils, the latter being mainly used by artists who execute their work on easels and who thus tend to get tied up in the search for minute detail. On being closely examined, the painting is clearly in an excellent state of preservation, barely restored and devoid of added touches.

31. - DAVID, FORMERLY CALLED APOLLO (*National Museum*)

Formerly called Apollo, Michelangelo carved the statue in 1530 on behalf of Baccio Valori. Giorgio Vasari has this to say of it: « ... In order to make a friend of Baccio Valori, he began to carve a statue in marble, three arms' length in height, which he called Apollo and which he depicted drawing an arrow from his quiver, all but completing it. Today it is to be found in the Prince of Florence's bedchamber, an object of rare grace, even though not entirely finished ».

At a later date it was transferred to a niche in the amphitheatre of the Boboli Garden, and then to the Uffizi Gallery, prior to being placed in the National Museum. The movement of the figure, the bold slant of its posture and the characteristic marks left by the claw-tooth chisel should be noted.

32. - BACCHUS (*National Museum*)

During his first sojourn in Rome lasting from 1496 to 1501, Michelangelo carved on behalf of one Messer Jacopo Galli, a wealthy Roman merchant, a life-size statue of *Cupid*, and also one of *Bacchus* in a drunken state. The latter, described in detail by Aldrovandi, was later sold by Paolo Galli to Prince Francesco of Tuscany for two hundred and forty ducats. In his right hand Bacchus holds a drinking-cup, while in his left is the skin of a wild animal and a bunch of grapes which a little satyr, grinning maliciously, is in the act of snatching away from him. In this fine, classic-style work of Michelangelo, his search for formal elegance is clearly evident, as is the case with the Madonna della Scala in the Buonarroti House Museum, just as his customary superhuman plastic vigour is lacking—all the more so in his delicate, almost effeminate moulding of the young ephebe's torso and chubby face. Bacchus, drunk through copious libations, sways and staggers, almost falling over backwards in his search for something to lean on, his bloodshot eyes staring fixedly at his cup filled to the brim.

33. - BUST OF BRUTUS (*National Museum*)

In or about 1540, Michelangelo gave the bust to
Tiberio Calcagni, his favourite pupil, in order that
the latter might complete it. However, for unknown
reasons it was never finished.
The manner in which the bull neck is set on the broad
shoulders covered by the toga is indeed admirable, as
is the expression on the proud face of the notorious
Roman.

34. - MARTYRDOM OF ST. ANDREW (*National Museum*)

A small unifinished work, well roughed out and
rich in pathos, to which it is difficult to give an
exact date. From the centre of the rectangle the
cross, bearing the transfixed Saint in his agony,
dominates the whole.

35. - MADONNA AND CHILD WITH ST. GIOVANNINO (*National Museum*)

The tondo belonged first to Bartolommeo Pitti and
then to the Guicciardini family. The Madonna is
depicted sitting on a large stone holding the Child
Jesus in her arms, behind whom appears St. Giovannino. The face of the Virgin stands out to a
greater extent than the other parts of the bas-relief, carved using the customary claw-tooth chisel
technique.

33

34

35

36. - VICTORY OF VIRTUE OVER BRUTE FORCE
(Palazzo Vecchio)

The work, commissioned from Michelangelo by Pope Julius II della Rovere, belongs to the series of statues destined to adorn the tomb of the latter.

Following the drawing up of the first set of designs for the tomb, to which the Pope had given his approval in 1505, though later reduced and modified, seven statues were excluded, namely, two out of the eight already roughed out by Michelangelo in Rome, and five begun in Florence. In the latter five statues, presented by Lionardo Buonarroti, nephew of Michelangelo, to the Grand Duke Cosimo I, was included the so-called group depicting the Victory of Virtue over Brute Force, together with a Prisoner, which today may be seen in the Hall of the Five Hundred, in the Palazzo Vecchio.

The group depicts a nude youth, who, with his left knee, presses against the back of an old man, while locking the latter to himself with his right leg. Thus held prisoner in the mass of the block, the old man, his head bent forward, is by now prostate and beaten, whereas his agile, powerful victor, from the height of his human pedestal, holds himself proudly, his piercing gaze sweeping over the field of battle round about him. On account of its small, though fine head and long, flexible, athletic body could this figure of Victory be compared in greatness of manner and execution to those in the New Sacristy. An expression of infinite sadness, contracted and twisting with agony, is visible in the face of the old man, who, with bent back, desperately attempts to throw off the weight of the yoke oppressing him.

In connection with this group, the various sketches drawn by Michelangelo for his series of Prisoners are of great interest, and today may be seen at the Ashmolean Museum, in the University of Oxford, England.

37

CASA BUONARROTI (Home of Michelangelo)

In his youth Michelangelo lived in the house standing on the corner of Via Anguillara and Via dei Bentaccordi. On the side overlooking the latter street, a memorial plaque bearing the following inscription was added in the 19th century: « The House in which Michelangelo Buonarroti, born at Caprese in the Casentino District, lived the years of his youth ».

On the other hand, the house at no. 70, Via Ghibellina, today a museum, was bought by Michelangelo on March 9, 1508, from one Benedetto Bonsi for the price of fifteen hundred gold florins. As to how long the sculptor lived in this house is not easy to say, though the period during which he was its occupant was certainly lengthy.

In due course, the house passed to Michelangelo's nephew, Lionardo, who later left it to his son, Michelangelo the Younger. The latter with great care restored the premises so that the few remaining works by his renowned great-uncle still remaining in possession of the family might be exhibited there for posterity.

By his will dated February 9, 1858, Commendator Cosimo Buonarroti bequeathed the house and all the works of art therein contained to the City of Florence. Whoever has the chance should visit the Museum, recently rearranged with excellent results.

37. - MADONNA DELLA SCALA (*Buonarroti House Museum*)

In the carved marble bas-relief the Virgin Mary is depicted in a sitting position, while holding the Child Jesus in her lap. In the upper part of the relief to the left are three *putti,* one of whom, leaning against the balustrade, is about to descend the stairs. Hence the name of the relief, namely, Madonna of the Stairs.

The work dates from Michelangelo's early youth, and though belonging to the same period as the one representing *Centaurs fighting,* it is more delicately carved and with details shown in greater relief. The influence of Donatello is clearly felt in the extent to which the various figures stand out in relief, as well as in the Virgin Mary's mantle and in her arms embracing the sturdy Babe, who, twisting as if to free Himself from her grasp, leans His head against His Mother's bosom.

The Madonna della Scala belonged formerly to the Grand Duke Cosimo I dei Medici who was very attached to it. In 1617 the work was given back to the Buonarroti family by wish of Cosimo II, following which Michelangelo the Younger placed it in the house of his great ancestor, together with other masterpieces by his hand.

38. - CRUCIFIX (*Buonarroti House Museum*)

Tradition has it that the Crucifix was commissioned from Michelangelo by the Prior of the Augustan Order, at the Church of Santo Spirito. In fact, following the death of Lorenzo the Magnificent, Michelangelo turned to the study of anatomy with such assiduousness that the Prior of the covent, who was both admirer and friend to him, allowed him to « skin » the bodies of patients who had died in the infirmary. The Crucifix, judged a fine work by Michelangelo's contemporaries, was placed in the choir of Santo Spirito; refound a few years ago, it was duly restored and the upper coats of paint, later applied to it, removed. While many critics are unanimous in maintaining that the Crucifix was made by Michelangelo as a young man, others have raised doubts in this respect, with the result that the matter is open to speculation.

39. - BATTLE OF THE CENTAURS (*Buonarroti House Museum*)

The relief was carved by Michelangelo in 1492 at the age of seventeen, the subject having been suggested to him by the poet Agnolo Poliziano. Giorgio Vasari writes of it thus: « A work of such fine craftsmanship that to the onlooker it appears not to be by the hand of a youth, but rather by that of an accomplished master proficient at his art and studies. It is kept in the house of Mi-

chelangelo, not only in memory of him but also as a rarity, by Lionardo, his nephew ».
In the bas-relief composed of twenty-six figures armed with large stones, the rendering of movement is superlative, while the subject-matter is treated with power and breadth—in truth the forerunner of the magnificent works later carved by Michelangelo during his long, troubled life.

40. - MONUMENT AND TOMB OF MICHELANGELO (*Church of Santa Croce*)

The monument to Michelangelo was erected by wish of his nephew, Lionardo Buonarroti. Permission to build it having been duly obtained from the Grand Duke Cosimo I dei Medici, Giorgio Vasari was commissioned to draw up designs for it, later receiving from the Grand Duke several blocks of marble required for its construction.
Once the designs had been prepared and approved,

Valerio Cioli was ordered to carve the central figure representing *sculpture*, while to Giovanni Bandini fell the task of making the one to the right, namely, *architecture*, whereas that on the left, *painting*, was assigned to Battista Lorenzi, who was also responsible for carving the bust of Michelangelo.
Work on the monument lasted from 1564 to 1570.

INDEX OF THE WORKS